Small Talk

Talk To Anyone And Be Instantly Likable

Gary Allman

not engaging in the rendering of legal, financial, medical or professional advice.

By reading this document, the reader agrees that under no circumstances are we responsible for any losses, direct or indirect, which are incurred as a result of the use of information contained within this document, including, but not limited to, —errors, omissions, or inaccuracies.

Table Of Contents

Introduction

Do you want to make more friends? Do you find yourself regularly wishing you knew what the right thing to say was but struggle to find the words you need? Have you ever contemplated if you would achieve greater success, either personally or professionally, if only you knew how to communicate with people more naturally? If any of these or other similar scenarios pertain to you, then this book will no doubt prove a valuable resource as you navigate the trials of day to day communication.

In this book, we tackle many of the most common pitfalls that occur when we attempt to make small talk. Techniques on how to communicate with strangers comfortably as well as methods on how to grow closer to acquaintances will be included. You will learn how to avoid conversation stagnation and how to keep a conversation flourishing. We will also discuss proven strategies on how to make almost anyone feel more comfortable around you to build a more fulfilling relationship with them.

Additionally, we will delve into tips and ideas on how to make a great first impression (and we will discuss how to ensure it stays great through the end of your talks). This book contains advice on how to break through your fears and insecurities in order to present a confident, amiable appearance and will guide you through both verbal and non-verbal behavioral cues that will allow you to read the body language of others and learn how to manage your own to your advantage.

Once you have completed reading this e-book, it is my fervent wish that you will come away with the knowledge and the confidence to start and carry on a conversation with anyone.

Furthermore, I hope it allows you to gain a deeper understanding of the people around you by way of enabling you to really get to know acquaintances, coworkers and other prospective friends or comrades on a deeper and more personal level. Finally, this text will strive to ensure that you finish it feeling more aware of your own words and actions and with greater confidence in yourself and a richer understanding of how to put your own best foot forward and truly show off your strengths.

Thank you for purchasing this book and have a pleasant read.

Chapter 1:
Techniques For Creating
A Stellar First Impression

To start any conversation off on the right foot and ensure that your speaking partners actually desire to converse with you, you must present yourself in a way that inspires others to want to talk to you. This can be accomplished in both verbal and non-verbal ways, a variety of which will be discussed in this chapter.

When it comes to making an exemplary initial impression, you must first and foremost consider your appearance and the reaction and impact it is likely to inspire in others. Obviously, there are many aspects of your appearance that you have little or no control over. Your skin, hair and eye color, as well as your height, overall build, and facial features are the product of genetics and biology, and there is not much you can do to change them regardless of how the general public might perceive them. But if so much is outside of your control does that mean making an effort is futile? Will people dislike you from the start based solely on your appearance? Fortunately for all of us, things are not quite that simple. While you cannot dictate how people will react to the appearance you were born with, there are many factors that go into formulating first impressions, which are well within your own control. These include your first few words or opening statement, your body language and the signals you send, be they conscious or unconscious, and the elements of your physical appearance that you can directly modify to create a fantastic first impression, such as your outfit and your hairstyle.

We will discuss the first thing people will notice about you before you ever have the chance to say a single word: your appearance. It might be shallow to judge someone based on how they look but nearly all of us are guilty of it. Stereotypes about people who dress or look a certain way are alive and well, and you must contend with the possibility that you are being stereotyped for your looks whenever you interact with anyone whom you do not know very well. To some extent you cannot prevent this but by focusing on the way you dress you can definitely influence how others will perceive you and can likely subvert any negative stereotypes they might prematurely hold against you simply by choosing clothing that gives off a positive and confident vibe.

So, what fashion choices will cause others to like you? Well, this all depends on where you are and who you will be talking to. You have no doubt heard the old saying "dress for the career you want, not the one you have" and you will find this idea will apply in almost any social arena, not just career based ones. In general, dressing in a pulled together, and professional or business casual type wardrobe will work well, though of course this can be altered to suit your own personal style. Additionally, feel free to tailor your wardrobe to the activity you are doing and the people you will be chatting with there. A formal dinner certainly requires a different outfit choice than a pool party, and it would look very strange at either event if you reversed the wardrobe choice. It is also important to consider who you will be talking to primarily. An elderly conservative individual will likely perceive you differently than a twenty-year-old art student will so dress accordingly.

In addition to ensuring that you dress to impress your intended audience, there are some general rules of appearance that will work when engaging nearly anyone from any demographic or age range. These are basic things that can be easily overlooked if you are in a hurry or otherwise distracted. Ensure your hygiene is up to snuff and that you smell pleasant or at the least, inoffensive. Make sure that you are well-groomed, with well-brushed hair, clean nails, and no lint or stains on your clothing. If you have trouble finding outfits that fit you in a flattering way, considering finding a good tailor or learning some sewing skills of your own. Well- tailored clothing can work wonders for ensuring you present yourself in a positive light.

Just as important as the clothing you choose to wear is your body language and facial expressions. In the chapter that follows this one we will delve into the nuances and meanings of various motions and poses but it is so important when it comes to ensuring that your first impression is a good one that it is worth mentioning here. If you have hunched or closed off posture, you will not appear as friendly or personable as if you stand in an upright manner. Take care to not cross your arms over your body too much as that can make you appear as though you do not want to talk to anyone. Finally, be aware of your facial expression. While there are certainly social settings that call for a serious demeanor, in general when you meet someone new, smile! Studies suggest that people instantly like you better when you smile, and they will form a higher opinion of you and be more willing to engage you in conversation. You never get a second chance to make a first impression but by dressing and behaving in a friendly, approachable and distinguished manner, the people you hope to impress will perceive you as confident, charming, and personable. This enables you to comfortably break the ice with them and move smoothly into a conversation not marred by negative judgment based on your appearance.

Chapter 2:
First Impressions in Various Scenarios – Job Interview

These are the basics you need to keep in mind when you want to create a good first impression. Let us, now, take a look at some common social scenarios and how specifically you can go about creating a good first impression on people in such scenarios.

We generally prepare for job interviews by imagining all the tough questions that could be thrown at us, or the funny yet professional things we can say to lighten the atmosphere or even the best responses we can give to the simplest questions. Yet, before you even start answering these questions or indulging in witty banter, you need to remember that all eyes are on you from the moment your resume hits their desk to the moment you walk out of the room, interview completed. It's a series of first impressions here and you need to make sure that you ace each and every one of those first impressions. Here's how you can do it.

a) **Be Punctual**

Remember, you're better off showing up early than showing up on time. In today's fast paced world, no one has the time to wait and making anyone wait is considered the height of bad manners. After all, a lot of people believe that time is money; by being late you're making them waste their money. It also creates the impression that you will always have trouble showing up on time, completing work on time, making it in time for deadlines and so on.

Instead, if you feel that you might have trouble with being on time, try to schedule getting ready as though your interview is an hour earlier than it actually is. For example, if your interview is scheduled at 10 a.m., set your alarm and prepare for it as though it were at 9 a.m. This gives you ample time to deal with anything that might suddenly come up and make you late, such as an unanticipated traffic jam. If you do get to the interview venue an hour before time, you can then take the time to go have a cup of coffee or go over any notes you want to in preparation.

If you are going to be late, make sure that you call your interviewers and let them know what's going on. Don't make them wait for twenty five minutes and then show up and make an excuse. Even if it is true, the excuse will sound lame.

b) **Dress Appropriately**

As we discussed earlier, how you dress does play a major role in how you are perceived, especially when someone is meeting you for the first time. This goes double at any job interview. Unless you're interviewing at a company where the dress code is casual and wearing a suit makes you come across as stodgy or stuffy, a suit is your best bet at any interview. However, just wearing a suit isn't enough. Make sure that your suit is neat, clean and well-pressed. Your shoes should also not have scuff marks.

At the same time don't carry too much. Do you really want to be the person juggling papers, a purse or a briefcase, an umbrella and the door all at the same time? It may make for some funny movie moments; it's less humorous in real life.

c) **Essentials Only**

While many consider coffee an office staple, walking into the room with a paper cup of coffee isn't how you want to start things off here. Imagine the impression you create when the first thing you ask for is a trash can! The burger or bagel you were eating or even the gum you're chewing – they all need to go before you step in to the building. While these things may not lose you the job, they don't exactly make the best first impression.

d) **Manners are for Receptionists too**

While the receptionist is not the human resources person or the hiring manager you're supposed to meet, that doesn't mean that you can afford to ignore them or, worse yet, behave badly with them. Many companies ask the attendants at their front desks for their impressions of the interviewees. Those impressions also play a role in the final decision made by the company. Besides, if you do get the job, this is going to be someone you interact with on more or less a daily basis. Do you really want to start out on the wrong foot here?

e) **Put Away Your Phone**

While seeing someone engaged on their smartphone is a pretty common sight – after all, people pull out their phones whenever they have a minute to spare – it may not be the best idea to start scrolling through stuff on your phone while waiting for your turn. Instead, you can take this time to go over what you know of the company, or what you want to say in the interview or even go over your resume. What you don't want is for the interviewer to walk out and for you to hurriedly be closing Candy Crush Saga and trying to push your phone out of sight.

f) Make Sure Everything is within Reach

You know that quite early into the interview, they're going to ask you for a copy of your resume, or your references. They may even need you to sign something or mark something or take notes. This means that these things have to be within easy reach for you. You should be able to open your bag and take out whatever you need. Don't show them that you needed to wade through a bunch of stuff – papers, old receipts, keys, candy wrappers and other detritus before you could retrieve the necessary items. Once again, these may make for funny cinematic moments, but they make you come across as messy and ill-organized.

g) Move First

Since you're technically the guest at the interview, it makes sense to believe that the host, your interviewer, should make the first move when introductions come up. This doesn't mean that you cannot extend your hand first for the introductory handshake. When you do this, you put forth the impression that you're eager to be there and are ready to begin your interview. It gives an impression of confidence and self-assurance.

h) Connect

After the introductions are done, try to find a point of commonality between the interviewer and yourself. Look around you and see if there is anything you can use. For example, if you see a photograph of the interviewer at a ski resort and you know something about it, (skiing or the resort or both) comment on it and ask them how they enjoyed their trip there.

If you can't find anything that could work as a conversation starter, dig a little deeper into the small talk. Ask about how long the interviewer has been in this town, where they moved from and so on. Try to find out details that will give you that connection. A minute of chatting about it will put both you and the interviewer at ease and help pave the way for a more relaxed interview.

Chapter 3:
First Impressions in Various Scenarios – Networking Event

Networking events are the perfect venues to make contacts, regardless of whether you are looking for new business opportunities or a new job. First impressions matter a lot here because if you don't stand out from the crowd, chances are that you will be easily forgotten. You need to ensure that people remember their interactions with you and they do so for all the right reasons. Here are some ways that you can prepare for and make a good first impression at networking events.

Research

It is a very good idea to do some homework before you attend the event. Find out who is speaking at the event, who will be attending and what the itinerary is. These bits of information are generally released some time ahead of the event, so you have time to prepare yourself.

Figure out if there is anyone in particular you would like to hear that day or any specific people that you want to meet. Apart from the itinerary, another great place to get this information is social media, such as the Facebook event page, if one has been created.

Keep Your Business Cards Ready

Even in the age of digital contacts a business card is the most professional way to exchange contact information. If you don't have any, have them made up. The look of the business card itself can be based on whatever it is that you do, but ensure that you have plenty.

Having a business card saves you the embarrassment of having to hunt around for pen and paper to jot down your details. What could be worse is that such a piece of paper might be easy for them to throw away after some time. You could have them take the details down in their phone but aside from being a bit too pushy, it is not an effective reminder. A business card, on the other hand, reminds people of you and the event they met you at, which can be very useful for you in terms of business or a job.

Elevator Pitch

Remember that at a networking event, you don't have the time to give people the whole your business plan and your entire life journey. They need a condensed version that gives them an overview of who you are, what you do and most importantly, how you can help them. This is your sales pitch, but it's a lot more than that too. It's your bio and brand statement in a nutshell. The wording, however, should be memorable and something that delivers a punch since you'll be giving this out verbally.

To put together an elevator pitch, consider why you're creating one. Determine what the purpose behind the pitch is – to get you a job, to get investment or to market yourself as a consultant. Then answer questions such as, what value you give, what makes your offer unique, how you provide the value and what your target market is. The answers to these questions should make for a pretty effective pitch.

Be Smart in Your Turnout

Again, as discussed in previous chapters, shallow though it is, the fact remains that appearance matters. A networking event is a professional setting. How you present yourself at such a venue determines how others will see you. Not just your clothes, but your hygiene and grooming can make a difference in how people judge you. After all, would you like to stand close to someone with a bad case of body odor?

Generally, a dress code is given for such an event so make sure you adhere to it. If you don't know the dress code, determine what type of an event it is, what your field or industry is like and what you think that people will want or expect you to wear. A good rule of thumb here is that if you aren't sure, be over dressed rather than under dressed.

Be Conscious of Your Body Language

We have already discussed body language briefly and what impact it creates on people around you. While we will go into more detail in later chapters, at a networking event you need to be very conscious of how you hold yourself. The fact is that such events can be daunting because you're going to meet a lot of new people and are naturally nervous about creating a good impression. However, don't let your nervousness show.

As we said earlier, arms crossed across the chest can give out the message that you are closed off to the people around you. It also comes off as a defensive posture, leaving people to wonder why you feel you're under attack. Instead, keep your posture straight but not rigid and your stance relaxed and open. You want to project confidence and approachability, not standoffishness and defensiveness. As a basic rule, smile and make eye contact with people around the room. Smiles work wonders!

Focus on Others, Not Just Yourself

What's the most boring conversation you've had? Chances are it's one where one of the people went on and on about a topic that seemed to fascinate only them – themselves. It is tempting, isn't it, to give in to the urge to talk about yourself? However, if you want to make a good impression you need to turn the focus from you onto others. This is not to say that you have to be reticent in any way or not put yourself forward. Just don't spend all your time talking about you. Listen to others, focus on them, encourage them to talk about themselves and you'll have their attention in a way you wouldn't believe.

Chapter 4:
First Impressions in Various Scenarios – First Date

You get only one chance to make a first impression. Nowhere is this adage truer than it is on a first date. Naturally, you'll want to present yourself in the best possible light to ensure that things go favorably. It's not that difficult to do this and get a second date. Be considerate and polite to your date, display an interest in them and ensure that they enjoy their time with you. Honestly, that's all it takes to attract your date to you and create a great first impression.

Look Presentable for Your Date

Basic hygiene is a must. Think about it; would you like to go on a date with someone who has body odor issues or someone who shows you what they had for dinner last night, just by smiling? Take care of your basic hygiene. This means that a hot shower is indicated. Brush your teeth and wash your hair before your date. Make sure that you are clean, smell fresh and good and look presentable from the skin outward.

Remember, making yourself look and smell presentable is only the first step. You'll feel more confident when you look and smell clean, but you'll feel even better when you smell good. Use a mouthwash to rinse your mouth and don't forget the deodorant. Make sure that the deodorant isn't overwhelming though. It may seem like a lot of work right now – although, it really isn't – but you won't regret it when you get close to your date.

Dress Smartly and Appropriately

Make sure that what you wear isn't dowdy or ill-fitting. Find clothes that are striking and look good on your figure or enhance it. Also keep in mind where you're going for your date. After all, you don't want to dress up in smart but casual jeans for an evening at the opera. If you are planning to attend the opera, you'll need a proper suit or evening gown. Otherwise, based on the venue, you can go for a neatly pressed pair of khakis with a button down shirt or a cocktail dress or smart blouse and skirt. Whatever you wear should be at once stylish and comfortable. Remember, it isn't about just looking good but feeling good too.

If you're meeting up for a light lunch or even just coffee, don't bother getting all dressed up. As mentioned earlier, decide what you'll wear based upon where you're going. Color always brightens things up, so wearing something with it is always a good idea. Bright colors make you seem bold and vibrant, as per studies conducted.

Style and Groom

A clean up and a good outfit are absolutely necessary but looking presentable doesn't just stop there. Your general appearance also includes things such as hair, nails and in the case of men, beards and/or moustaches. Make sure that your hair looks neat and well-groomed. Gentlemen, keep your beard or moustache (if you have one) trimmed and neat, too. Cut your nails if necessary. Ladies, that would mean that a manicure and a pedicure is in order. Chipped nail polish is not attractive.

It's a first date, so it is safe to assume that your appearance will be examined quite closely. After all, you'll be doing the same with your date. Keep this assumption in mind while getting ready and you won't miss anything. A spray of a delicate perfume or understated cologne is a good idea, but don't empty half the bottle on yourself.

Smile

Be ready to smile a lot. It is natural to feel nervous and uncomfortable, but try not to let is show. Smile and act as naturally as possible. Smiling makes you seem attractive to your date. It also does wonders for your own mood.

Research shows that when you smile you radiate positivity and others feel as though they can trust you. Of course, it also lets people know that you're a fun person. As mentioned above, smiling also helps ease your own nerves when you start feeling edgy and, perhaps, just a bit jittery before the date or while on the date.

Plan an Interesting Date

A first date can be nerve-wracking enough without having to sit and think of things to talk about to keep the conversation going. Most people go out for dinner or a movie or both on a first date, but if you feel that that is too intimidating or too much pressure, you have other options. You can try a new bar, go for a long walk, get tickets to a concert or show or game that both of you enjoy or even enjoy a quiet picnic. You can even attend a cooking class for couples if that is what interests you.

It's not uncommon to feel a lot of pressure on a first date; after all, you're expected to make interesting conversation for hours with someone who is, for all intents and purposes, a perfect stranger. When you do something that doesn't just involve talking but doing things together, both of you can relax. You'll find that conversation is much smoother and an unusual activity makes for a date that both of you will remember for the right reasons.

Punctuality is a Must

If you've fixed seven as the time for your date, don't show up at seven-thirty. If you've committed to a time for the date, stick to it. It is also a good idea to check with your date if he or she is going to meet you at a pre-arranged location or whether you will pick them up or be picked up by them. Don't cut things too fine in terms of time. Make sure that you've taken care of any last minute details before you set out.

Try to arrive a little bit early for the date. Don't be too early, though. You don't want to seem desperate. Arriving five to ten minutes early shows that you are serious about the date. If the venue is new to you or if you are nervous or both, you can use this time to acquaint yourself with your surroundings and mentally

Politeness is Key

Being friendly is great, but something that can make your first date easier and more comfortable is good manners. Consideration always earns good marks. If the lady is ok with it, the gentleman should observe small courtesies such as picking up the check, opening doors and pulling out chairs. Ladies can also show some consideration by offering to go halves on the bill. Good manners put the other person at ease and help you avoid situations that could make them and you uncomfortable.

Don't do anything blindly. Be aware of your date's reactions to small gestures to see whether they receive them favorably or not. Not all ladies appreciate having doors opened for them and not all gentleman appreciate going halves on the bill. Don't force it if they don't want it. Consideration extends to not forcing good manners down their throats.

Don't ask clichéd questions

Nervousness about getting to know someone new can affect conversations. It is not uncommon that conversation during a first date begins to sound like an interview for a job. Asking your date about their hobbies, work and personal beliefs is fine but don't just stop there. Topics such as family, friends, favorite movies, books or music, enjoyable vacations and pets are all good ways to learn more about your date and to keep the conversation going. Try asking something unusual such as what they would do if they found out the world was going to end in a few days.

This is not a police interrogation either. Be tactful when you ask them about their preferences. Past relationships are a big no-no; frankly, it's none of your business. Work stresses are only to be talked about if they show an interest in talking about such a topic.

Show that You're Interested in Them

Give all your attention to your date. Show that you are genuinely interested in who they are and what they're saying. Eye contact and verbal confirmations such as 'uh-huh', 'yes' and 'I agree' are good ways to let them know that you are listening to them.

One of the biggest complaints that people have about a first date is that their date ends up taking over the conversation. If you find this trait annoying, you definitely don't want to emulate it. Conversing with someone is very different from being the only one doing the talking. Pay attention while they are talking and put in your two cents worth when the conversation is directed towards you. Gauge your date's mood throughout the conversation and be mindful of things such as whether they're comfortable and whether you may be talking too much.

Having a Good Time is Most Important

While going on a first date can be quite stressful, don't treat it as an obligation. Remember that under all that nervousness, you have asked for or agreed to the date, so you must be anticipating a good time too. Focus on that instead of the butterflies in your stomach. Try to have as much fun as possible and maintain a positive attitude. Entertain your date so that both you and he or she keep laughing. While you do want to make a good impression, don't start taking the date so seriously that you lose any sense of humor. It's inevitable that a part of your brain will try to keep analyzing the date while it is happening, but try to shut it off or at least don't listen to it. Relax and enjoy your date's company. After all, that is why you are here.

Make sure that your expectations of the date aren't sky high and that your motives are exactly what they should be – getting to know your date. Anything else and the date could become uncomfortable. Enjoy getting to know them and spending time with them.

Sometimes, if it feels as though the date isn't going as well as you thought, don't be afraid to change the situation a bit. For example, if your date looks bored at the opera, ask them if they would like to leave and suggest a few drinks at a fancy bar instead. Merely changing the environment can go a long way in making things less stressful and helping you enjoy each other's company.

Find Common Ground

In your conversation with your date, try to find out what both of you have in common and work on that. For example, if both of you enjoy trying out different cuisines, you can ask them for their opinion of a restaurant both of you have been to. If you enjoy the same type of movies, discuss those movies in detail if you want. Finding out what you have in common and working on it goes a long way in helping you connect more deeply with your date. Conversation also becomes much easier since you can talk about a lot of different things now.

Similarities are great but sometimes opposites work even better. If your date doesn't like something that you do, don't immediately decide that things won't work out. Sometimes their differing viewpoints will give you an insight into who they are and where they're coming from. You might find that an opposing opinion actually facilitates a better conversation than merely exploring similarities.

Ask for a Second Date

Once the evening is over and if the date has gone well, ask them if they would like to see you again. Let them know that you enjoyed spending time with them and had a good time. You can give them your phone number and ask them to text or call you. You can even ask for their phone number if you feel that they wouldn't mind giving it to you. A good first impression leaves the door open to you forming a connection that could end up being abiding.

Don't push it with the phone number – either yours or theirs. First, gauge how your date felt about your encounter. If your date has enjoyed it, asking for the phone number or offering your own is ok. Once you have the number, ensure that you call the other person or text them to tell them that you enjoyed yourself with them, within a couple of days.

Chapter 5:
First Impressions in Various Scenarios – Public Speaking

Within the first few seconds of being introduced to someone new, a person makes at least 9 conclusions, according to one Business Insider report. That means that before you even open your mouth to speak, some audience members may have decided if your presentation was worth listening to or not. With so many decisions being made at the start of any meeting, the pressure to make a good first impression is critical.

While these tips are mostly for public speakers, people in the corporate world can use them too. For CIOs and other IT leaders, giving presentations can sometimes be one of the hardest parts of the job. However, as the role continues to transform, the need for top notch presentation skills is becoming more important. Below are eight ways to make a lasting impression on your next pitch.

Speak Slowly

The biggest mistake that most new speakers make is that they talk too fast on the stage. Of course, it is totally apparent why this happens. After all, you are new to this so you will be apprehensive and edgy. You will also be trying to remember everything you have to say. The general feeling is one of – "Let me just finish this presentation so that I can get off the stage. I don't want people staring at me and judging me anymore." Believe me, I can understand that. However, what actually happens is that in your rush to finish everything, you end up actually rushing through your speech too fast. This makes it difficult for your audience to actually comprehend what you're talking about.

Here's a rule of thumb that can help you:

Slow down when you talk. A good indicator of how slow you need to go is when you start feeling uncomfortable about how slow your speed is. A generally accepted maxim is "Speak half as fast as you think you need to". Practice speaking slowly and on the big day, try to slow down.

Be Conscious of Your Body Language

As we have discussed in a previous chapter, your body language or non-verbal communication can be quite important. Here are a couple of reasons why it is important in public speaking.

Verbal communication isn't the only means of communication that we pick up on. Non-verbal cues that include your body language can either complement verbal communication or give the lie to it. Your verbal communication can be strengthened by things such as your posture, how you hold yourself and even the way you gesticulate with your hands.

There can be things that you are doing without realizing that they don't help your cause. Nervousness can make us do things that we are not conscious of such as wringing our hands or pacing too much or too fast.

Here's a list of nervous behaviors that you would do well to keep an eye out for:

- Moving back and forth on the stage too fast and slightly aimlessly

- Tapping your feet

- Touches to your face or hair

- Fidgeting with objects such as pens

- Putting your hands in your pockets or fiddling with other parts of your clothes or with jewelry

- Constantly rubbing the nape of your neck

- Checking your slides far more than you need to

- Swinging your arms back and forth

Try to figure out what gestures you make unconsciously when you are nervous and get rid of them. Also try to use gestures consciously for dramatic effect. This can allow you to get the audience's attention and keep it – in a good way.

Make Eye Contact

Another mistake quite a few new speakers make is looking only at one person in the audience or one section in the audience or even not looking at the audience at all. Remember, everyone present, whether they're sitting or standing is part of the audience. You are there to address all of them, not just one part. Don't avoid eye contact.

At regular intervals, look at different parts of your audience. Make sure that you cover your entire audience during your presentation. Make eye contact with as many people as possible and allow it to last for at least four to five seconds before moving on. Of course, I can understand that you might find this intimidating. Nervousness about being on stage is not made any better by adding this thing about eye contact, is it?

If you are feeling nervous, though, here is a simple trick that you can use:

Look at the people in the back row and look above their heads. If the room is large enough, they'll be too far back to know whether you're looking directly at them or not. This way you can keep moving your head without actually having to look at anyone and home in on different parts of your audience.

While this trick might make your life seem easy when it comes to public speaking, it is better for you to challenge yourself. When you next go for a talk or a presentation, try to look directly at a few audience members, at least. As you do this more and more, it gets easier. It also has the added advantage of making it feel as though you are speaking to each individual member of the audience and not just the people in the back row.

Practice, Practice, Practice... Ad Infinitum

Practice as much as you can. The aim here is to practice until you can't go wrong. Make sure not only that you know your material inside out, but also that you thoroughly know how you're going to present it.

You may forget things in the heat and anxiousness of the moment. However, if you have mastered all your material this is much less like to happen. Actually knowing that you know the content of your talk or presentation thoroughly can actually help you be less anxious than you would be if you weren't very well prepared. A lot of confidence as a speaker comes from knowing exactly what you're planning to say.

This is where you'll probably tell me that your public speaking trainer or teacher told you never to memorize your material. They're not wrong. You don't want to write down the whole speech and mug it up. Delivering such a speech will only make you sound as though you're reciting it or reading it out.

The goal here is to be able to get on that stage and to deliver your talk or speech without having to keep looking at note cards. One of the best ways to do this is to write out your speech or talk in bullet points. Remember to include every main point, important fact and clarification. When you practice the first few times, keep these bullet points in your hands so that you can refer to them whenever you need to. The more you practice, though, the better you'll know your material. Soon you'll be able to recall the details and have them form a complete image. When you reach this stage, practice without the bullet points.

Keep doing this and you'll know all your material from A to Z. When you go up on that stage, you won't use the exact same words that you used during the practice sessions, but that's not important. What matters is that your delivery will be confident and practiced.

Once you have done this, you'll see that practice isn't just good for any individual speeches. It is also great if you want to improve your performance as a speaker in general.

A local Toastmasters group in your region may provide you with the perfect setting to practice your skill at speaking. If you are in college, you can also take a speech class to improve your public speaking skills. Also, observe and try to emulate some of the speakers on forums such as Ted talks.

Film Yourself

A great way to ensure that you get everything you can out of your practice sessions is to film them.

As I mentioned earlier, nervousness can make us do things that we're not conscious of. A great way to figure out what to avoid doing is to find an empty room and repeatedly practice your speech. During these initial sessions, don't worry about how you're presenting; this is the time to know your material and become well-versed in it. Once you're confident of the material, film each practice session. View it before moving on to the next practice session. This helps you to home in on things you may not have even noticed that you were doing such as speaking too fast, fiddling with clothes or other objects, looking back at the slides too much and so on.

Figure Out How Your Audience Sees You

In my experience, most audience members fall into one of two categories.

The first category is the supporters. These are people who are ready to listen to you, interested in your topic and want you to do well at your speech.

The second and not so great category is the bored people. As the name says, these people aren't too thrilled about being there. They aren't thinking about you and your speech. They are distracted and you probably won't be able to reach them no matter what you do.Please note that neither category of people is going to curse your name, boo you, throw rotten eggs or tomatoes at you or heckle you off the stage. That's the one thing you must recognize. The supporters will support you through the good and bad parts of your talk and will forgive any mistakes you might make. The bored people won't care one or another. Their opinion of you is not important, because they don't want to be there in the first place. Don't worry about how they might react during your speech. Chances are they aren't even thinking about it. That is not on you so don't let it affect your performance. Once the talk is over ask for and take into account any constructive criticism that you get. Incorporate it in future practice sessions and actual stage appearances.

Focus on Your Topic, Not on Your Performance

When you're planning out and writing the material for your speech, home in on what you want it to do and how it should affect the audience. Figuring out exactly what you want to deliver to your audience helps make the talk appear much less intimidating. You no longer worry about whether you have something in your teeth, or whether you're looking back at the slides too much or even whether your body language is 'right' or not. It becomes more like explaining things to a friend and less like an actual speech in front of a vast audience.

Perfection Is Not the Goal

There is no such thing as the perfect speech. Let me give you an instance. I was supposed to give an hour's talk on a competitive exam to some professionals. I had one of my colleagues sit in on the talk so that they could let me know what I may have missed out or not done very well during the talk. At the end of the session, my colleague praised my performance highly and couldn't find any faults. I, on the other hand, was able to pick out at least three things that I could have done differently or better.

You are your own best or worst critic. You'll find that no performance of yours will ever satisfy you completely. However, aiming for perfection will only end up crippling you by making you more anxious than you need to be. It's best to understand one thing up front – your talk isn't perfect and that's alright.

Author and speaker Scott Berkun has this to say:

"I don't want to be perfect. I want to be useful, I want to be good, and I want to sound like myself."

Your speaking should help you achieve these qualities. In fact, this should be your goal in whatever you do. Forget about being perfect – no one is. Instead, take a deep breath, go up on that stage and just be yourself.

Chapter 6:
First Impressions in Various Scenarios
– First Day on the Job

So you've just started your dream job. After the celebration is over and all the wine drunk, how can you make sure that you make the right first impression in the new office. After all, no one is in a hurry to get fired in the first few weeks or months – or ever.

You may be able to forget that you're the new kid on the block, but people around you won't. You need to ensure that you pay attention to the culture at work and so what you can to make sure that your entry into your new role is as smooth as possible.

Here are 10 tips that you can use to make sure that your first impression at your job is a good one.

Be Open to Guidance and Advice

Rosalinda Oropeza Randall, the author of Don't Burp in the Boardroom and an expert at workplace etiquette says that making the right first impression is very important. A lot of this first impression is influenced by what you say.

In an interview with Business Insider, she said that being open to a new way of working is one of the most important things to remember at a new job. She also says that being humble and willing to learn creates a good impression. What does not create a good impression is saying things such as "In my last job..."

While bringing previous experience and knowledge to your new workplace is great, don't make comparisons to the methods used at your old workplace – especially ones that are favorable to the old and not quite as favorable to the new. Show that you are open to new ideas and new ways of doing things, not just stuck in the old ways.

Volunteer

First of all, become familiar with your job. Next, check with your superior to make sure you are on the right track. Then, ask for additional opportunities in your company.

Volunteering for new tasks or roles or even committees demonstrates qualities such as willingness to work with a team, and, of course, leadership. However, remember that this is in addition to your regular position; don't let it take over your new position. Most importantly, keep checking with your superior from time to time to ensure that you're doing all that's expected of you before you take on something new.

Be Content With What You Have

You've just started the new job. No matter how well you work or what your ultimate ambitions are, this is not the time to start asking for more such as a raise, telecommuting, a different schedule or other such demands. You should have negotiated a salary that's fair and any other benefits at the time of accepting the position. If you have decided that what you have isn't enough or doesn't fit with your circumstances any more, wait for the first performance review. If you can prove, at that time, that you can do a great job, it'll be safer for you to bring up requests for any changes you may have in mind.

Do Not Get Involved in Gossip

You might have a quirky colleague you'd like to know more about. You may even want to know who is involved in office politics and how. No matter how curious you are, though, do not get involved in the office grapevine. Most especially, do not voluntarily ask about things such as who is having an affair with who, who you should avoid and so on.

It is good to get to know your colleagues, but do it in a professional manner. Conversations should be about work and a little bit of small talk when you are new to the office. Randall said to Business Insider that you should "take time to meet and engage in small talk with each person in your department. Judge for yourself."

Upgrades Are for Later

If you get a phone, software or computer from work and you don't quite like it, keep quiet. This isn't the time to complain about it. Later, once you're more comfortable and settled in, you can talk about upgrading what you've received, but right now you need to make do with what you have. Once you've proven that you are a valuable and stellar employee, you can ask for a better office chair or laptop.

Don't Criticize Your Previous Job

As I mentioned earlier, it is a bad idea to compare working practices unfavorably to your previous job. The opposite end of the spectrum is true, too. You may be tempted to relate horror stories about how your old boss ran amuck, how a huge contract was lost thanks to an incompetent colleague, or even your feelings about how you felt they treated their workers.

Don't give in to the temptation. This can only reflect badly on you, especially if you are new. Remember that people in your industry will find out what you've been saying about them. Not only is it unkind, but also unprofessional. You may also be hindering any future opportunities with this kind of talk.

Be On Time

Knowing what the company culture is where punctuality is concerned is very important. This doesn't just mean what time your hiring manager tells you to show up at on your first day, although that is important too. But there are unspoken rules of punctuality vis a vis company culture that you need to know about.

For example, if the office hours are 9 to 5 but everyone keeps working until 6, don't overlook this. In your early days at a new workplace, you need to follow the flow. Do what your colleagues do. This means staying back as long as they do. Not doing so can give you the reputation of being someone who likes to skip out early. In the first few days, it is best to be cautious. Keep looking out of your workstation to see where everyone else is.

Dress Appropriately

Of course, in most places, you won't show up to work in a t-shirt and ripped jeans. But this does bring home the dilemma of what to wear. If you are confused or uncertain about what the dress code is, simply ask.

When you're new, it behooves you to take a little extra time over your appearance so that you look smart and put together. This does not mean that you need spend a lot of money on buying a whole new wardrobe. What it means is that your clothes should be neat and clean, you should be well-groomed and you should follow the company's dress code.

Ask Questions – Avoid Repetition

It is only natural that, at a new job, you need to some time to find out how everything works. Don't be afraid to ask questions. Asking how to do something is better than messing it up and having to do it all over again, just because you didn't ask.

At the same time, pay attention to what you're told. Don't ask the same questions again and again. Asking questions to find out the best way to do something is great; having those instructions repeated to you again and again makes you look needy and incapable.

Use the Lunch Hour for More

At lunchtime, it is tempting to keep to yourself by having a sandwich at your workstation or using this time to run errands. However, when you're new, this is the time you can use to get to know your colleagues. Sit down and eat with different colleagues or go to the park to join coworkers who eat there. At the same time, remember what I said about gossip – it's a strict no-no!

While doing this, ensure that you are cognizant of company culture. If there is heavy workload and everyone is grabbing a bite at their workstations, this isn't the time to look for lunch dates. As mentioned in the point about punctuality, do what your colleagues are doing.

Chapter 7:
What Your Non-Verbals Are Saying About You

As we touched on lightly in the previous chapter, non-verbal communication, including your facial expressions and body language, can say a great deal about you. Once you are aware of what messages you are sending subconsciously, you will be able to tweak your non-verbal communication to suit whatever vibe you are trying to project. Additionally, understanding the meaning behind non-verbal cues will enable you to better read those you are communicating with. Once you can determine how they are responding, you can tweak your own speech to better suit your audience.

Think about what sort of body language you normally adopt in social settings. How is your posture? Do you routinely cross your arms and legs? Are you fidgety? These behaviors cause you to appear uncomfortable, closed off and ill at ease. Stand straight and tall, shoulders back. Ideally, keep your arms in a relaxed position at your sides. Crossing them over your chest or playing with your hair can create the wrong impression. Don't be afraid to gesture naturally during the conversation, though. This makes it clear that you are engaged in your conversation and passionate about what you are saying.

When you are seated, make sure to maintain good posture. You can cross your legs, but it is noteworthy that crossing them with your foot pointing towards your chatting companion is superior to the reverse, as it implies that you are enjoying their company. Ensure you do not position yourself in such a way that you take up multiple seats, making it hard for others to sit down beside you. Do not put your elbows on the table or otherwise lean on it too much; that could be perceived as impolite, and that is what your seat back is there for.

While communicating with others make sure that you use physical touch appropriately. A firm handshake upon being introduced is usually called for, and there are other times throughout conversation, depending on the relationship or intended relationship with your conversational partner in which a light touch on the arm or shoulder can be welcome and aid in creating a more intimate setting. Keep in mind that this will work best if the conversation is more emotional or personal, enabling you to reach out in a comforting manner. Alternatively, a flirty or suggestive conversation can be benefited by a light touch, basically in situations which intimacy is warranted and natural. Any sort of physical contact, besides handshakes as a greeting and a goodbye, is very likely to be out of a place in a more business-like setting and should be used with extreme caution lest they prove detrimental. If you do have a conversation in which it feels natural and appropriate to use physical touch as a part of your non-verbal communication, be on the lookout for your partner's response. Some people are naturally uncomfortable with being touched by those they are not close to and it will not enhance a bond if you force someone to engage in something they would prefer to avoid. Used correctly, however, engaging in handshakes, hugs, and light touches can cause others to respect you more and feel closer to you. Just consider the time, place and nature of the interaction before you proceed and you will find physical contact to be a useful tool throughout your conversations.

Besides just your body language and what to do with your hands, it is important to consider what your facial expression is telling people. No matter how pleasant your words may sound, people are unlikely to be convinced of your cheer if you cannot say them with a smile. Of course, it is not as simple as just smiling during conversations. It tends to be a wise decision during greetings and farewells, but it will not always suit the mood of the conversation at hand. In a business meeting, interview or other more serious interaction, a somber or studious expression can work wonders. You will want to take care in any conversation; you may have to not look bored or uninterested when it is someone else's turn to speak. Be a good listener and ensure that shows during your conversations. Nod at the appropriate times, laugh when it suits the story. Really listen to what the people you converse with have to say, even when it is not a topic that interests you very much. If you show that you care about what they have to say, they will be much more inclined to care when it is your turn to speak and the impression they form of you will be vastly improved, no matter the time, place or subject matter.

Chapter 8:
Tools To Break Through Fear And Break The Ice

Often, the greatest setback to any of us being fantastic conversationalists is our own fear. What if we say the wrong thing? What if someone does not like us? All too often we are so afraid of failure that we do not even attempt to start a conversation. It can be hard to ever truly stop being afraid, but it is okay if you stay scared. What matters is that you go ahead and start that talk anyway, even if you fear how it will end. You can never succeed if you do not even try, and you cannot let fear hold you back from friendships, opportunities, and a fulfilling social life. In this chapter, we will discuss a variety of tactics that you can employ to push past your fear and finally work up the nerve to ask for a promotion, invite that cute guy or gal out for coffee or simply say hi to someone new that you might have a lot in common with. After all, what is the worst that could happen?

One method to get past the fear is to hype yourself up. Instead of focusing on all of the negatives, consider the positives. You might get the raise you have been working so hard for. You could make a new friend, set a date or just have a really nice conversation with somebody new. You have a lot you could offer, after all. You are a fantastic listener if you want to be (and you should want to be!). If you are reading this book, you likely want to know how to converse better, which means you are a probably friendly and want to get to know people. Maybe you are smart, kind or funny. What do your current friends like about you? What do you like about you? What makes you special, interesting or worth getting to know? Focus on those things and ignore the fear that someone might not like you.

There is a lot to like about you, and there is a lot to be gained by pushing past your fear and actually talking to somebody else.

Another thing to keep in mind when you are scared is that the vast majority of us will feel this way at some point or another. Public speaking is an extraordinarily common fear shared by many of us and initiating a conversation goes hand and hand with that intrinsic terror. You are not the only one who is afraid of rejection, of failure, of someone not liking you. It is in fact very likely that if you are trying to convince yourself to break the ice with someone new that they are grappling with the very same fear of approaching you. People rarely discuss this with others, because we all feel that we are the only one going through it but it is a very common human reaction, and you are not alone.

Finally, I would like to propose a non-conventional strategy to take that first step and talk to somebody. If you cannot manage to stop focusing on all the negative things that could occur from breaking the ice, then go ahead and address your fears. What is the worst that could happen? They deny your request for a raise, promotion or date? Well, that is nothing you cannot brush off. At least you tried and at the end of the day, you are back where you started and have in reality lost nothing. Maybe you tried to start a conversation or get to know someone, and they brushed you off and did not like you. That's okay too. Not everyone will like you, and you will not like all of them. You found out a prospective friend was not someone you clicked with after all, and now you know. Not everyone will give you what you want when you make requests, and not all conversations with new people will prove fruitful. Perhaps you will find out you have nothing in common, or you will discover that you disagree on matters that are very important to you, or you simply will not enjoy conversing with one another. This person is not going to go home and spread hateful rumors about you. They will simply move on with their life with no good coming from your efforts, and you can do the same. Pick yourself back up, remind yourself that nothing truly bad came of it and try again at the next opportunity. Rejection is frightening for almost all of us, but it is not as bad as we make it out to be inside our minds. The only true personal failure occurs if we never try at all.

When you are eventually ready to take that first step and talk to someone, do not overthink the first words you say too much. Meeting someone new? A simple "Hi, I'm 'insert your name here.' I noticed 'common interest/other notable feature' about you. I'm really interested in that as well and thought I would take a minute to introduce myself. May I ask your name?" will usually work wonders. If the person in question is a new coworker, classmate or is in some other way new to a routine activity that you now share, this becomes even easier. "Hi, I'm 'your name here.' I noticed you are new here and wanted to welcome you to the 'company/class/neighborhood.' If you have any questions, feel free to ask me!" Be friendly, easy going and to the point. Allow them to end the conversation if they are busy or uninterested but leave an opening for them to feel comfortable talking to you again and do not hesitate to greet them and engage in friendly small talk when you see them again. Depending on their initial response, you might be able to plunge into deeper conversation from the start, but we will delve into the intricacies of moving past simple pleasantries in a later chapter towards the end of this book. Taking that first step is frequently the hardest part, but I think if you try the steps suggested here you will find it surprisingly simple, although still frightening. The good news is that the more often you practice these skills, the less scary it will become, and you will no longer lose out on friendships due to fear.

Chapter 9:
Strategies To Seal A Memorable Verbal Impression

So how can you ensure that people will remember you after you have worked up the nerve to introduce yourself? What can you do to be certain that your new acquaintances will be comfortable greeting you or initiating conversation in the future? What about a brief chat with you can make you stand out from the many faces we all encounter in a day or week?

This can be difficult to answer since it is a multi- faceted conundrum. Take a moment to reflect on traits that cause you, personally to remember someone a day or two after you met them. They would likely have to stand out from the norm in some way but if you are not careful standing out is all too easy to accomplish in a negative manner. If someone smells funny, gets a bit too touchy, is far too emotional or cold, you might very well remember them but the odds of you chatting with them again if you can avoid it are rather low.

Fortunately, there are ways you can endeavor to make yourself stand out in a positive way. Besides appearance and nonverbal communication, both of which can make a difference in sealing the impression people form and keep of you, what you say matters. This does not mean you have to choose entirely complex words but makes your choice something that suits who you are. That can be accomplished by choosing fancier words or by focusing the conversation on an eclectic (and ideally mutual) interest or simply by being a fantastic listener. People remember those who made them feel special, valued or important. If you are not comfortable standing out in other ways, the simplest method is to listen studiously, with the appropriate comments and nods, to what your conversational partner is saying.

If you are more willing to venture further afield and put yourself out there, you might consider sharing something unusual with your new acquaintance. A hobby, collection or interesting and distinctive fact works well here but keep it at a casual, appropriate level, nothing intimate or ethically questionable. A fun and amusing anecdote, story or habit can strike someone's interest and make you stand out from the sea of people they have spoken to that day. This works even better if you can work in a way to figure out a fun fact about them and remember it for the next time you chat.

Finally, you can simply make your conversation a bit more unusual than the standard fare. If you have a (natural) accent or favor unusual word choices, you may already be more easily remembered. With that said it is not worth faking such a thing if it does not come naturally, there are easier and more honest ways to distinguish yourself. For instance, when you run through the generic small talk conversations, be more specific than you need to be. Do not simply ask what your chat partner thinks of the weather, mention the upcoming storm or how cold or hot it has been lately and take the time to ask them what they think about that sort of weather. Do they come from somewhere that is similar or different and do they like it? Take the time to flesh things out a bit beyond the basic requirements and people are very likely to remember the pleasant chat you shared well after your initial introduction.

Chapter 10:
How to Make Small Talk

Small talk isn't small, no matter what one might think. You may think that talking about the weather is clichéd, but many a great relationship or friendship has started over shared frustrations about this innocuous subject. Small talk isn't just a means of filling in uncomfortable silences. It is a way to build bonds with people and a skill that can be absolutely vital in the professional arena. If you want to become an expert at small talk, here are some steps you need to keep in mind.

Make Your Body Language Approachable

If you want someone to feel comfortable around you, pay attention to your stance. Don't come on too strong, but do move your body towards the person. Make eye contact, turn your torso towards them but don't cross your arms over your chest. Don't stand too close or too far. Doing all this will make the person feel as though you're interested in what they have to say and aren't just tolerating them.

Another non-verbal cue that makes people feel you're not paying attention is constantly looking at your phone. It gives the impression that what you're looking at there is more interesting than what they have to say.

At the same time, give the other person their space. As I said earlier, don't stand too close. Look eager to listen to what they have to say, but not so eager that it borders on manic. You don't want to scare the person away.

Have a Friendly Greeting Ready

Your greeting depends, of course, on whether you know the person or not. If it is someone you're already acquainted with a simple hello followed by his or her name will do. For example, "Hey John, how are you?" It's direct and simple and let's them know that you're interested in talking to them. If it's someone you're meeting for the first time, start by introducing yourself. It'll help you feel confident. You can say something like, "Hi, I'm John. May I know your name?" Once the introduction is complete, repeat the other person's name; it's a great way to remember names and it makes them feel special.

Smile when the two of you are talking and ensure that you pay attention to them when you greet them. Do not look bored or perform perfunctory introductions as though you were just waiting for someone more interesting to show up.

Talk Lightly and Positively

You exchange energy in a conversation just as much as you do information. To ensure that you have great small talk that can lead to a great conversation, keep things fun, positive and light. A positive and upbeat attitude and a willingness to laugh at funny parts of the conversation, especially when they're about you, makes another person want to keep talking to you even when you're discussing something as mundane as the weather.

Of course, fun and light is difficult after a bad day at work or at home. However, if you're engaging in small talk with someone, chances are they aren't a close friend. Letting go and complaining about how bad your day, week, month or year has been will only succeed in turning them off.

Begin with a Compliment

Start with a basic compliment such as, "I really like your skirt – where did you get it?" Before you know it, you may be involved in a fun conversation about retail therapy. Don't be disheartened if the conversation doesn't immediately take off, though. You've still appreciated something about that person, which will make them feel good about themselves and therefore, about you. They will be more receptive to other subjects that you talk about. If you're feeling a bit leery about leading straight in with an introduction, you can use this as a way to introduce yourself.

Figure Out What You Have in Common

Establishing common ground doesn't just mean that both of you are fans of the same sports team. Something as commonplace as having the same bad experiences with traffic that day can be used to discover common ground. Common ground is simply a way to establish what both of you can relate to, so that a connection can be formed. You may find the weather too innocuous or cliché to talk about, but remember that you can build up to the stuff that matters once you have established common ground. Here are some ways to do this:

"Isn't Professor Duncan funny?"

"Don't you just love the parties that Justin throws?"

"Did you also get stuck in the rain today?"

"Glen's Kitchen is one of my favorite places to hang out."

Open Up a Bit about Yourself

Now that common ground has been established, you can use it as a basis to open up a bit about yourself. This doesn't mean that you tell them something intensely personal that will probably scare them off such as, "I'm so obsessed with Professor Duncan." However, you can use this opportunity to talk about yourself a little bit more. Here are some ways to follow up on the statements in the previous point:

"I enjoy his classes immensely. He makes archaeology sound like fun."

"I met Justin last week when I was doing an interview with one of the other players."

"I tried to set out early to beat the weather, so I could get to the gym but I was too late. I had to spend the next one hour in traffic."

"I find that it's the best place to hangout with my friends. The music isn't too loud so you can hear yourself talk and they do a mean pizza with barbecue sauce."

Engage the Other Person

Establishing common ground and opening up about yourself is just one step. Now you need to bring the other person into the conversation. You can do this by asking them to yield some information about themselves. Don't ask intensely personal questions such as their viewpoint on religion or politics. Keep it simple and fun. Ask questions about their job, interests or even surroundings. Here are a few ways to engage another person:

"What about you? Are you interested in archaeology too, or do you enjoy his jokes?"

"Have you been to any of Justin's parties before or are you attending one for the first time?"

"Did the rain keep you from something fun today?"

"Do you come here to hang out or for the food?"

Ask a Question or Make a Statement

Your next step will depend upon how the person responds. Below are a few ways to keep a conversation going:

Other person: "Oh, I'm an archaeology student too. Duncan's a bonus, but I've always wanted to be an archaeologist."

You: "Really? What drew you to archaeology? It's great to meet someone who is as interested as I am in this field."

Other person: "It's my first time attending one of Justin's parties but I've heard of them. I heard the Halloween party was a blast."

You: "Oh it was! So how do you know Justin?"

Other person: "I like the rain but not when I'm planning to head out for a movie. Missing that movie was a real letdown."

You: "What movie were you going for?"

Other person: "I love the food here. While I enjoy the pizza, I especially love their mushroom pot pie."

You: "Oh yes! The mushroom pot pie is delicious. Have you tried out any other dishes they make?"

Use Your Surroundings

Once the conversation really gets going, you can look for cues around you if you're stuck about what to say next. Use anything that you see – from what they might be wearing to posters on the wall. Here are some examples:

"This Coldplay t-shirt is so cool. Did you enjoy the concert?"

"Hey, you participated in the Ironman too? When? How was that experience?"

"Do you think this rendition of Macbeth will be good? I've been wanting to see the play for some time."

"Oh wow! You're reading 'The Picture of Dorian Grey'? Doesn't that book have interesting things to say about man's true nature?"

Listen Carefully to Them

Paying close attention or 'listening actively' to what the other person is saying can give you more cues about how to make the conversation lively and productive. If you hear a small comment that has the potential to take the conversation in a new direction, use it. Here are a few examples of how to use tangential cues in a conversation:

You: "I met Justin while holidaying with some common friends in France."

Other person: "Justin told me about that trip. He actually wanted a few lessons in French before setting out on it, although I don't know how much French he actually ended up using."

You: "Do you speak French? That is so cool. Where did you learn it?"

Other person: "My mother is from Quebec actually, so her first language is French. I learnt it at her knee. It's very different from the French spoken in New Orleans though, isn't it?"

You: "So I've heard. I believe that some expressions that are completely harmless in Parisian French can be considered quite offensive there. But I love the Fat Tuesday the best! New Orleans can be so much fun right?"

Other person: "Oh yes! It truly believes in letting the good times roll."

You: "Have you ever been there? How was it?"

Reveal Something of Yourself, Not Everything

By the time the conversation ends, you could have told the other person a bit more about yourself such as your volunteer work at animal shelters, how much you like videos of Gatsby the dog, or even how you feel about the latest Oscar winning movies. The person leaves having gained an insight into you that can forge a deeper connection and doesn't make them believe that the conversation wasn't important to you.

At the same time, though, be careful about how much you say. This isn't the time to talk about your political or religious views, your love life or your latest existential crisis.

If the Conversation Goes Well, Suggest Meeting Again

If the conversation has gone well so far, you will probably want to follow up with this person. This is when you can ask for their number or whether they want to hang out again.

"I would love to go see that play with you. Could I have your number so we plan it out?"

"I've never met someone who has enjoyed Fat Tuesday as much as I have. Do you want to hang out again so we can talk?"

"Will I see you at Justin's next party? I hear the theme is New Orleans so it should be quite a blast."

Farewell Pleasantly

After the small talk is over and you have to go, ensure that you leave the person feeling important and not as though you were just passing the time with them. Here are some ways to say goodbye politely and nicely.

"I had a lot of fun talking to you. I'll let you know how my next trip to NOLA goes."

"I'd love to discuss the book further but I see a friend who's about to leave."

"There's a classmate, Julian. Do you know him? Come with me and I'll introduce the two of you."

Chapter 11:
How To Make Your Personality Shine

Once you make it past the introductions and the first few generic conversational lines, you must find a way to distinguish yourself from others who might, at first glance, seem rather similar. We touched on this some in the previous chapter by discussing ways to make sure you are memorable and create a lasting impression on those you talk to but how can you enable new acquaintances to know more about you on an individual level?

If your newfound potential friends never learn anything distinctive about you, due either to your own shyness or to conversations simply never getting passed the most mundane of topics, it is unlikely that you will ever develop a deeper connection with them. There would simply be no way for them to know if the two of you have anything in common worth pursuing, any shared interests that you may want to delve into a deeper conversation about one day. They will be unaware of your strengths, your weaknesses, your quirks and your charms. Of course, this is hardly information you need to display openly to anyone and some traits might very well be best kept firmly under wraps until true intimacy is established but revealing select tidbits that might prove interesting can allow you to build and enhance new friendships by opening up about yourself. In turn, your new companions will be more inclined to do the same, possibly revealing shared eccentricities, interests or lifestyle choices that you can enjoy and/or discuss together in more detail.

Often, the biggest detriment to letting others see glimpses of our personality and interests is due to shame. What if they dislike those features or interests, and we simply embarrass ourselves? What if they consider the information we share out of place or too forward and everything is awkward between them and us forever? All too often we convince ourselves that the things we like and our own personalities will not be liked by others, but the only way to know is to let prospective friends know about these things. If you hide them, you will be rather bland since none of your best personality features or fun interests will be shown at all. You will also eliminate the chance of learning if they might enjoy similar pastimes or share your quirks and that would be a shame because shared interests and features are a surefire way to trigger bonding and a memorable impression.

As for technique on how to accomplish this, it is actually fairly straightforward. If something comes up that interests or excites you, simply mention it. Ask your acquaintance their thoughts on it and share yours. In this way, you can discuss skills, hobbies, even qualities you possess or value in others in a relatively organic way. Be careful not to force your viewpoints upon your chat companion. Express yourself in an enthusiastic but non-judgmental manner. You might discover that you have a lot in common, but the reverse could also happen. Even if you discover that you have little in common with the person who was so recently a stranger, it will do you little good to burn bridges or create an enemy. If you discover that your opinions diverge in a manner too significant to move past pleasantly, change the topic or if you must, politely end the conversation. If on occasion someone does hold different values or simply does not seem to share any of your interests, do not take it personally. In many cases, if you approach such people with flexibility and genuine interest, you might find that you have more in common than you thought or at the very least you will gain an interesting new perspective. Ultimately, no harm is likely to befall you from making your own interests and personality traits apparent, the worst case scenario, you simply both move on, leaving your own mentalities firmly intact. In other scenarios, you may be able to enjoy conversing with even someone with very different viewpoints from your own once you understand the reasoning behind them. Do not let fears of shame, judgment or rejection keep you from letting others see who you really are. It is the only way you can have valid and legitimate conversations with others, and that is worth the relatively minor risk incurred.

Chapter 12:
How to Develop Your People Skills

As any person does, you'll have to interact with different people in different ways – something that continues all your life. Interpersonal skills are important in any interaction, whether it be a shopping trip, making new friends or leading a team. I'm sure that you've realized by now, how crucial communication skills are to success. You've probably also recognized that some techniques of interaction are better than others. If you want to develop your people skills or interpersonal skills, you'll need to work on your image, your methods of interaction and your non-verbal communication.

Understand What Constitutes Non-Verbal Communication

Non-verbal communication, as the name implies, is everything that doesn't have to do with the words you speak. It can include how you touch, what your facial expressions are like and how you sound. In this context, people rely more on visual cues than they do on audio cues and therefore, visual cues become more vital to successful interpretation. Even in visual cues, people are more likely to look at facial expressions rather than body language to determine what you are trying to convey.

For instance, if you want to convey happiness, a smile is more effective than a faster rate of speech or exuberant body language. Similarly, hiding a facial expression makes it easier for you to hide how you are feeling at that moment, if you don't want to show it – if you're afraid of something, for example.

Understand How Crucial Non-Verbal Communication Is

Non-verbal communication is supposed to make up around 60% of interpersonal communication. In order to make sure that your non-verbal communication is successful, you need to be able to convey your emotions in a manner that others can discern accurately.

You need to carefully consider the non-verbal cues that you display while engaged in a communication. While doing this, also think about the non-verbal cues that you get from other people and think about what you pick up from these cues.

Master Body Language that Makes Others Comfortable

The kind of body language that sets others at ease differs from culture to culture. For the purposes of this book I will talk about Western culture. Your face and body should be directed at the other person and you should lean forward a bit towards them. You can also use gestures and variations in your volume, vocal pitch and rate to convey your feelings. Show that you are listening carefully to them by smiling, nodding at what they say and, most importantly, not interrupting. Be alert but relaxed, as well.

This means that your shoulders should be straight but your muscles should be relaxed. At the same time, if you find that you are thinking too much about your body language, focus on what the other person is saying, instead.

Discern Cultural Differences

Understand that body language does not work the same way in different cultures. What is a sign of respect in one culture could be considered quite offensive in another. A good example is that of burping. In Western culture, burping at any time is considered very bad manners and even disgusting. However, in some Middle-Eastern cultures, if you don't burp after a meal, it is considered a grave insult to the host since it implies that you didn't enjoy the meal.

Obviously, the non-verbal cues of the culture that you belong to will be instinctive for you. However, if you need to communicate in a culture other than your own, observe others to discern what the normal non-verbal cues are. It may also be a good idea to read up about such cues.

Determine How Gender Differences Influence Non-Verbal Communication

While trying to understand and interpret non-verbal communication, one of the factors you must consider is gender differences. Non-verbal cues are displayed very differently by men and women. In general, women are believed to be more likely to make eye contact, smile and be open to touch – whether giving it or receiving it. They also listen more and interrupt less and can discern facial expressions better than men can.

Manage Your Emotional Cues

For successful communication, you must be able to regulate the emotional cues you display. This becomes especially important when you are in the grip of strong emotion. At such a time, it's best if you breathe deeply and try to find a calm centre. If you are sending out tense signals through your body language, try to relax the language. Don't clench your fists and relax your muscles and your jaw. Studies have shown that those who can control and manage their emotional cues are more likely to gain trust from others.

Set Goals

Review your interactions and try to determine if they are getting you the results you want. Try to determine whether you were able to achieve your goal in that conversation. Do you think the other person understood you and what you wanted? If the answer is in the negative, you will need to strategize your communication skills.

Persuade, don't order: Logic is a very useful tool when you're attempting to persuade someone to do something. For example, if you want to persuade your roommate to take out the trash this time, you can point out that in order for both of you to do the same amount of work, he or she needs to take out the trash this time as you did it last time.

Make your body language welcoming: If you feel that the response to a request is not favorable, try using open body language as discussed earlier. Also attempt active listening.

Listen: don't try to take over the conversation. Keep an eye on your responses and how you listen to the other person. Use verbal cues such as "mmhmm", "really" and "go on" to indicate that you are listening.

Be assertive, but in a strategic manner: Use 'I' based messages rather than 'you' based messages. Instead of talking aggressively, for example, "You are upsetting me..." try using an assertive message such as "I'm feeling upset..."

Make Your Communication Efficient

Don't use complicated and indirect messages when a simple and direct message will do. Try to plan and practice what you want to communicate whenever you can. This ensures that your message is delivered easily and quickly. Efficient communication skills don't just allow others to comprehend what you want to say but also allow you to communicate more in the same amount of time.

For instance, if you want to ask someone to do something for you, don't beat about the bush. Instead of saying, "If you see fit and if you have the time, would you be willing to do something for me" say, "Could you please do this for me?"

Let Others Talk

Everyone wants to be involved in a conversation. You need to be comfortable with silences that last a few seconds so that you can allow others to talk. The hallmark of a competent communicator is his or her ability to focus on the person they are conversing with.

You can try noticing how long you've been talking in a particular conversation. If you've been saying your piece for some time, wrap it up and pause so that the other person knows that it's their turn to talk.

Understand What Constitutes Good Conversation

Effective communication has five principles – relevance, informativeness, truthfulness, modesty and politeness. People assume that your speech will do at least some of the following:

- add new and previously unknown information

- add elements that are interesting and relevant

- tell the truth, unless you use devices such as irony or sarcasm

- be polite

- not be boastful and bombastic

Don't Presume or Assume Things

Again, clear and direct communication avoids any misunderstanding. Presumptions or assumptions only cloud the message and mess up your relationships. For instance, if someone elderly asks you to repeat something that you said, don't straightaway assume that he or she is hard of hearing and start speaking louder.

Ask for clarification before moving on. You could say something like, "I'm sorry. Was I speaking too softly or too low?"

Don't Force A Conversation

Everyone likes to feel that they have a choice. As such, try to avoid forcing someone to go in a direction you want, or do something you want through forceful conversation. Remember, persuasion and direct communication are the keys to a successful conversation.

For instance, if you have made plans with a friend to go out and the friend has to drop out at the last minute because of a pet emergency, don't guilt your friend into continuing with the outing. Instead, express your disappointment and then be a good friend by offering to help.

Chapter 13:
How To Go From Introduction To Intimacy

Okay, so at this point you are probably aware of steps you can take to overcome your fear, take that first step and talk to someone. You should also now be knowledgeable of some of the strategies you can employ to make a memorable first impression showing off a taste of your interests and personality. But how do you communicate with someone past the first few interest getting lines and basic introductions? What enables people to move into more personal conversations and learn more about one another?

We will tackle the issue of how to take the next step past simple introductions with your new acquaintances in this chapter. If you have been following previous lessons, you will find that it is simpler than you might originally have expected. At this point in your conversation, you will have finished introducing yourself, perhaps pointed out something you found interesting about your new acquaintance and engaged in no more than a few sentences about relatively mundane things. From here, try to find a way to naturally spurn the conversation forward. If there is something pleasantly distinctive about your potential friend, ask about it. Compliments work well here but are too closed to ensure a good conversation. Do not just tell them you like their outfit but ask where they got it and if they regularly enjoy fashion. If something about their appearance or accessories suggests a shared interest, ask about it in a curious and enthusiastic manner now.

Moving to a more intimate stage is even easier when you are speaking to a coworker, classmate or anyone you met in a shared social event. You clearly have something in common binding you together. Ask your new colleague how they are enjoying the job so far and what they did before coming here. Asking classmates what they are studying is a common equivalent and for both groups of people you can ask them what they like (and even what they dislike) about their current or future line of work. Share your own feelings on the matter as well when it is your turn to speak. If you are at a recreational or leisure class or event, ask them how much experience they have with what you are doing and how they got into it in the first place.

If you are attempting to communicate fully with a stranger with whom you have no known like interests or tasks, it will take longer to build a connection. Ask simple and inoffensive things that can help you find shared things and show an interest. Are they from the town you are in and if not, where did they come from? In either case, do they like it here? Depending on the flow of the conversation, it might be natural to ask them briefly about their family or what they recommend doing for fun around the area. Step lightly when asking more personal questions, though, especially of someone who is more or less still a stranger to you. Read their body language and alter your questions if they appear uncomfortable. Do not be afraid to apologize if you feel you may have overstepped at some point. In doing so, you will show that you are paying attention to and listening to them and that you care about their comfort and happiness.

No matter how you meet someone, you can rest assured that the majority of people enjoy talking about themselves. Even if your initial conversational points are quite mundane, gently prodding for more information using thoughtful follow-up questions will usually enable you to get a conversation flowing and when that occurs you are likely to encounter a shared interest or trait. When you find one, mention it and ask for further information on their perspective on it. Very soon the conversation will flow naturally as two or more compatible people discuss a shared passion, and you will rapidly find yourself moving past mere introductions as you speak as friends do.

Chapter 14:
How To Revive A Dying Conversation-
And Keep It Alive

You managed to introduce yourself, find some shared interests and begin a conversation but eventually find it fizzling? Do you find your talks plagued by awkward silences before one or both of you mutter an excuse and slip away? Many of us have learned the social mores that dictate how to start a conversation; say hi or introduce ourselves but we frequently struggle to know what to say after, the more or less required script has been completed. We know that we need to say something to keep the conversation progressing but words fail us, or we are met with short answers and sent right back to where we started. In this chapter, we will focus on ways to revitalize a tapering conversation before it dies. If you follow the advice found here, you will be well on your way to enjoying lively and animated chats without the tense and uncomfortable silent stretches so many of us dread.

One surefire way to lessen long lulls in conversation is to simply avoid asking questions that can be easily answered with a simple yes or no. As you converse, you will naturally ask things of your conversational partner so word your questions in a way that ensures you are not asking yes or no questions. For example, do not ask something to the effect of "Do you like it?". Instead, reword that to "What do you like about it?". Once they answer that, you can ask them what they dislike about it as well. Additionally, alter your own answers to ensure you do not simply say yes or no to things. If the situation is turned around and your chatting companion asks if you like something, do not simply tell them that you do or do not. Take the time to elaborate on what and why. This will aid you in getting to know one another on a deeper level and will also greatly diminish the time and effort you have to spend in uncomfortable silence. Rewording your questions and your answers save you from having to continually churn out fresh yet natural feeling conversational ideas and lessen the chance of you accidentally bringing up something embarrassing or out of place in desperation. Conversations flow more smoothly, and you can learn much more about what triggers or motivates your new acquaintance, building rapport and deepening the connection you will begin to construct as you converse.

Another method of keeping your conversational spark alive is to ask questions and start discussions that can easily segue into diverse but related questions and discussions. If you begin a conversation about a job you share, you can start simply with what you like and dislike about it, but there is no reason to stop there. You can ask about what got them into that career in the first place and what other jobs they have worked in (and what they enjoyed and did not enjoy about those). If they changed their career, you could ask them what inspired that alteration to their life and if they are happy with their decision. If they have remained consistent, you can ask when they decided it was what they wanted to do and what originally interested them about it. Was it what they had expected when they were in college or otherwise preparing for the field? Is it better or worse than they had thought it would be? Do not be shy about sharing your own experiences as well. While you do not want to make the conversation all about you, give and take is natural and sharing the events you have gone through yourself might trigger additional comments or questions from your chat companion. This is particularly natural when you share an interest or hobby but can occur even when your passions are rather dissimilar, as long as you each keep an open mind.

Depending on how much your acquaintance is contributing to your conversation question wise, you might be able to keep a conversation going for quite some time by simply parroting. If you find yourself conversing with a more skilled conversationalist than yourself, answer their questions in a more detailed manner than a yes or no and then ask them the same question. This shows that you are interested in their perception of the matter and not solely focused on yourself and relieves you of the burden of coming up with topics all alone. Additionally, it ensures that all members of the conversation have the opportunity and invitation to weigh in on the same subject. Hearing the opinions and perspectives of others on such things can help you determine if you share things in common and perceive the world in similar ways, as well as giving you clues about their personality that you can use to come up with more topics of discussion.

Chapter 15:
Ending A Conversation Positively

No matter how swimmingly your conversation is going, all good things must come to an end and eventually that will include your discussions. Sometimes, this can feel awkward, with both members of the conversation needing or wanting to tend to someone else but each of us feeling pressured by social norms to avoid being rude and cutting someone off. Fortunately, there are viable tactics that we can employ to ensure that our conversations conclude as smoothly as they started, and we will delve into those strategies in this chapter.

If you feel it is time to end a conversation, do so politely but firmly. In many cases a not entirely subtle sign that you need to start doing other tasks will work but if you have a particularly chatty companion mere hints might not work. You can certainly start with a nice and simple "While I would love to chat more, I really have to get going." You can be more specific here if possible such as tell them you have to go to work, an appointment or any other obligation that you were going to tend to before the conversation. Do not make excuses just to end a discussion so honestly divulge the reason behind the departure in an upbeat and friendly manner. If your chatting mate does not seem to grasp that by mentioning your need to go accomplish other tasks, you are trying to let them know that it is time to say your farewells, you will have to be a bit more direct. Remain cordial and do not grow terse with them but be firm if they continue talking. "I hope we can continue this conversation soon, but I truly must get some work done. I will talk to you again later." In many cases, you can then simply wave and head off in whatever direction you need to go. You want to ensure that they do not have a good opportunity to interject and keep you from ending the chat.

The methods discussed in the previous paragraph also can work wonders when both parties are aware that the conversation is at an end, but both feel too shy to properly end it. If you find yourself in a scenario where both members are dropping hints about all of the things that they still need to attend to that day and neither is simply saying goodbye, be the one to take that step. As before, be friendly but firm. Assure your new acquaintance that you would be delighted to continue your chat at another time but you both have things to do for the rest of the day, and you will, unfortunately, have to postpone such pleasantries for an alternate date or time.

If you are ever in an event where your conversation partner needs to go and excuses themselves, try to pick up on their own hints and conclude your conversation. Otherwise, things can sometimes grow terse, and there is a risk that you will be cut off rather bluntly while they return to their own affairs. Additionally, prolonging goodbyes and making someone feel pressured into continuing to talk to you is unlikely to leave them with a positive impression overall. They will feel annoyed and might also second guess themselves if they feel that they were rude by ending a conversation you were not yet ready to finish. When attempting to make friends and master small talk, it is preferable to avoid putting anyone in such a situation. If they seem like they would like to end the conversation, offer to talk again later, wish them well and go about your business. They are sure to appreciate it and think well of you going forward.

Finally, it is prudent to end a conversation before it becomes stale. If you are starting to run out of topic ideas and foresee awkward silences incoming, conclude the conversation while you are ahead. Even if you might like to communicate more, if you are out of content that naturally fits into your conversation and relationship level, it is better to end the conversation and talk again in the future. Your topic choices will expand as you get to know each other more, and even some rehashing will likely be comfortable for everyone and not overly stale. Additionally, if you sense a vastly different opinion in the conversation that could become potentially confrontational, or you inadvertently unearth an uncomfortable or overly controversial topic choice, you might be wise to conclude your chat before it becomes a debate. When you are communicating with someone you do not know too well, some cans of worms are not worth opening right away, lest you jeopardize a potential friendship or connection. If you are able to ensure that you finish your discussions before things get tense, boring or awkward, you are sure to have pleasantly concluded conversations for years to come, and that will be the ending impression of you that people carry with them, making them desire to speak with you again in the future.

Chapter 16:
How To Deepen The Relationship
With Future Interactions

After you have met someone and chatted with them a few times, you might be wondering how to create more intimacy and establish a deeper connection. Being comfortable saying hi to someone now and again is hardly adequate when attempting to develop a friendship, after all. The good news is that once you have powered through the initial steps, we discussed earlier, conversation will likely get easier and easier. After you have had the opportunity to chat with someone on a very casual and basic level a couple of times you can slowly but surely begin to dig deeper, discovering new things about each other and finally developing a real, lasting relationship that goes beyond simply having been introduced.

You might wonder how you manage to move past the passing acquaintance stage and into something more permanent, and we will discuss how to do exactly that here. It seems like a challenge but by the time you are ready to take these steps, you will have likely spoken to your prospective new friend enough times that conversation comes relatively easily, and you should feel comfortable when approaching them now.

Start slow when you are trying to enhance your relationships. Do not rush into deeper questions right away and wait to do so until it fits the conversation. Continue to discuss the same comfortable small talk topics you have come to know and love. Each of your jobs, the weather, established shared interests which are all nice, safe topics to reuse as needed. We have established in earlier chapters how over time you can learn about their family and where they are from which is already new information to form a potential bond over. As you chat more, be on the lookout for opportunities to ask about other details about their life or interests and to drop some information about yourself as well.

In addition to delving into new topics, it eventually becomes prudent to propose meeting up or hanging out sometime. This should ideally be at a neutral location. Choose the event based on what you already know or suspect about your new friend. If you know you share an interest; you will probably be comfortable asking if they would be interested in attending something closely linked to that interest. You can word requests to visit such an event in a way that puts no pressure on you. A simple "So, I heard 'insert event name here' would be in the area this weekend. Did you hear about that? Were you thinking of going?" can allow you to gauge their reaction and proceed accordingly. Hint dropping works here as well. "I thought I might check it out, but I do not really know anyone who is interested in it, and it likely will not be as fun all alone." and see what your chat partner has to say. If they seem wholly uninterested, drop the topic, though feel free to tell them how it went if you do decide to go. If they seem like they would like to go but are hesitant due to not knowing people or just not being sure if it would be worth it, propose meeting up there or going together and stress that it will probably wind up really fun with someone to talk to also in attendance.

If you do not have any shared interests that you are both aware of and can't easily invite someone to go, you can say there would be a significant expense; it is more of a solo activity, or it would feel too intimate, hope of developing a deeper connection is not lost. If you want more opportunity to interact with a coworker, classmate or even a stranger you would like to get to know better, you might have to be a little bit blunter. Pick something inoffensive, well liked and easy to cut short if things are not going well and make sure you do not word things in a way that they might misinterpret as romantic intentions (unless that is what you are going for). Something to the effect of "It has been nice chatting with you, and I would like to hang out with you more and get to know you better. It would be nice to make a new friend in the area! Would you be interested in grabbing a cup of coffee together sometime?" is simple and easy. Better yet, propose a day to do it on. This gives them an out if they would rather not attend such a thing without shaming you in the process. If you say a day or two that work for you, they can tell you they are busy if they simply do not want to come. Of course, they might realistically be busy so you can try again in later days or weeks but if they always prove busy, do not push the issue and simply opt to remain acquaintances and enjoy the talks you get to have. Once you are getting to know each other in settings neither of you is required or pressured to be in, you are already moving comfortably out of the acquaintance stage and into the deeper connection that represents true friendship.

We learned what you should do or say if a conversation starts to fizzle and how to smoothly end a conversation before things turn sour. There are many topics you can discuss if you avoid yes or no questions, as usually, your chat companion will usually have something to say that you can ask about further or share your own experience with. Making sure you both answer questions or discussions asked or started by either of you is also an excellent way to keep a conversation going longer, especially if you combine it with asking for more information that can lead to entirely new lines of discussion. Finally, we learned the importance of ending a conversation on a high note- never let it become boring, stale, awkward or angering. If the conversation is not going well or if one of you simply has other things to do, conclude things in a pleasant but firm manner without allowing space for argument. You will be able to continue your conversation in the future when time permits, and with renewed freshness and vigor.

For easy reference, we will include in the conclusion a bullet list of conversational ideas you can engage in with a stranger or acquaintance. This list is far from comprehensive - there are always many more topics you can discover. For the purposes of organization, we will begin with what are commonly considered very mild, inoffensive small talk topics and move on to slightly deeper (but still acquaintance friendly) options. Remember that it is important to know your audience and to understand the mood and tone of your conversations. While these are relatively safe and easy discussions to have and can enable you to get to know another person better, there will be times where they do not fit into a conversation organically. There may even be times when they could make someone uncomfortable, resulting in a failed conversation and a negative impression. Which ones to employ will come down to the individual conversations and interactions that you have, it is just a list to inspire you if you ever do not know where to begin. Without further ado, some excellent topic choices for your fledgling conversations:

The weather. Widely considered a boring conversational choice but can be surprisingly interesting and insightful. If there are a major storm or otherwise interesting or unusual weather changes occurring, it can be a good topic of conversation. It can also clue you into your acquaintance's preferences on climate and geography, which can allow you to get to know them better.

Current events. Be careful of anything overly political or highly controversial unless you know someone well. If you are not, a rift could be created that might not be easily repairable.

That said, news and events, either good or bad, can be a great source of discussion. You can share reactions and perspectives on things happening in the world and in your community at the time which might reveal similar (or vastly different) perspectives.

Career/Studies. In most situations, especially work or school settings, it is safe and comfortable to ask someone what they like or dislike about the job, how long they have been in the field and what they found interesting about it initially. In many cases, you will be talking to someone who is clearly in a shared profession, and this can be an easy discussion to bond over. It can also be very revealing of someone's early life depending on their work history and motives.

Location, location, location. Few people are offended if you ask how long they have lived in the town or city and how they like it. If they are new there, where did they come from originally and how does it compare? For long term dwellers, did they ever want to move? Do they like it here? If you are new yourself, you can even ask for recommendations of things to do in the area. If things go well, they might even agree to show you around!

Obviously shared interests. Naturally, you cannot know what someone enjoys just by looking at them but some things you might be able to detect that you share in common. Perhaps they have a child around the same age as your own kids. Maybe they are wearing a t-shirt representing your favorite band or television show. You might even meet or encounter them at a class or recreational event making an interest clear; yoga class, book club, and other similar activities make it quite obvious that you share a common interest. Discuss what got them into it and what they enjoy about it. This can easily segue into other related interests that you are somewhat likely to have in common as well.

Family/Relationships. Tread carefully here, as depending on other factors this can be sensitive waters but asking if they have family in the area is usually inoffensive. In many cases, you can also discuss relationship status and find out if they do or do not have children. Do not be pushy in this area and only bring it up if it works in a natural and comfortable way.

Activities you both might enjoy. This one can be tricky to implement without seeming too pushy or coming on too strong but if there is an event in your area, asking if they are going or what they think of it can be a good way to learn about new interests or lack thereof. Depending on how things go, you might even get the chance to see them there.

Naturally, there are many other discussion categories available to you but feel free to use this as a resource to help trigger some safe and pleasant ideas. If you follow the tips found in this book, I am confident that you will be more comfortable beginning conversations and keeping them going, from start to finish. Your confidence will increase, and your social circle will expand as you brave the initial fear of introducing yourself to new people. In time, it will most likely begin to feel natural, and you will wonder what you found so frightening in the first place.

At this point, the only real step left is to get out there and meet people! With most things in life, practice makes perfect, and that definitely includes a small talk and social skills. Present yourself in an appealing manner, keep an eye on your body language and expressions and project an assertive and friendly nature. You will discover that a lot more people enjoy your company than you previously realized.

Conclusion

Now we come to the end where we put together everything we have learned. It is my hope that you feel more confident and aware of how to make small talk with people and how to use those skills to build lasting, fulfilling relationships. You should now know how to make an excellent first impression that creates lasting positive memories in those you talk to. You are also likely better at reading the body language and facial expressions of others, and hopefully, you can now adjust and manipulate your own to hide your fear and give off the confident and assertive vibes you are trying to project.

I also hope that you feel better able to handle fear and shame. Rejection and not being liked are concerns for all of us, but none of us like every single person we meet. If you remind yourself that even if things do not pan out between you and your new acquaintance, you ultimately did not lose anything by trying. In fact, your efforts will always reward you with valuable skills in talking to others you meet- many of which will reap the results you actually endeavored to achieve. You will not share like interests or qualities with everyone you meet and sometimes a conversation will wind up not going anywhere. That is okay! Do not get disheartened if you cannot befriend every single person you chat with. Not all of them will have personalities and passions that complement your own, after all. Rejection can hurt but not trying at all guarantees you fail, and a gentle rejection due to simple incompatibility can be better for everyone sometimes. Failing is not an excuse to stop trying, but if you follow the tips we discussed here, you are highly likely to succeed more often than not.

We also discussed ways to add depth and intimacy to your mundane conversations, eventually enabling you to turn them into genuine friendships. This is done by listening to what your chat partner is saying, asking for more details, and bonding over shared interests or experiences. Even when one of their interests is something you are largely unfamiliar with, admitting that and asking for more information will grant you a relatively pleasant conversational topic. People enjoy talking about themselves, and your acquaintances will appreciate your listening skills if you can carry on even a conversation that is more focused on them. As time goes on, you will discover more things that you share and will become more comfortable together. Eventually, you will find yourself exchanging contact information and getting together to chat and do things together more frequently, building the foundations of a beautiful friendship.

I really hope that you enjoyed this book and feel ready to apply the skills and techniques we discussed in your day to day life. If you are willing to take a moment to leave me a review, I would appreciate it. Thank you for your purchase and for reading my book, I wish you many happy conversations in the days to come!

Gary Allman

Other Books from Gary Allman

Conversation: The Gentle Art Of Hearing & Being Heard

Learn How To "Small Talk", How To Connect, How To Talk To Anyone!

Problems keeping the conversation going?

Don't worry. Gary Allman will help you become a MASTER of small talk!

Now, answer this question: do you ever feel your mind going BLANK during conversations? And then you think of all the things you could have said later on? Just imagine how great would it be to never run out of things to say during parties or meetings, with hot girls or with powerful men!

Conversation - The Gentle Art Of Hearing & Being Heard is here to help! This book will help you save time, energy and money as it gives you all the most important techniques and strategies for you to open, connect and "small talk" with anyone you want.

In this book you will find:

How to keep a conversation going in a way that makes YOU sound Fun and Interesting!

How you can have topics come up by themselves: never run out of things to say!

Gary Allman's fundamentals and strategies to unlock your conversational potential once and for all

How to start conversations with strangers and approach people you don't know with unbreakable confidence....

... and much more!

You can have this power: anyone can become a master of small talk easily and quickly... you just need to unleash your inner conversation skills and apply the tactics taught in this book. It's time to go from being tongue-tied and unsure of what to say to have fun meeting people and getting to know them better!

This book will teach you how to listen and speak more effectively, avoid the most common conversational disasters, think faster on your feet, forget awkward silences and use proven strategies that allow you to successfully communicate your point of view to anyone.

So get your own copy of Conversation: The Gentle Art Of Hearing & Being Heard TODAY!

Trust yourself and take action!

Amazon.com link: http://amzn.to/1TV3C5c

Dirty Talk: The Psychology And Physiology of "Talking Dirty"

The Easiest Way to Mind-Blowing Sex for Men & Women

Gary Allman is about to revolutionize your sex life. Are you ready?

Do you ever feel **Awkward** or **Shy** when it comes to dirty talk? A lot of people feel uncomfortable when they first start talking dirty to their partner. And, let's face it, how can you possibly enjoy dirty talk if you're constantly worried about how you sound?

Dirty Talk - The Psychology and Physiology of Talking Dirty is here to help! This book will help you save time, energy and money as it gives you all the most important techniques and strategies for you to have the mind-blowing sex you deserve!

In this book you will find:

Simple words that will drive your man crazy. He'll stay harder and get bigger.

How to take control of your man the way you want to and never let him get away. Learn what every man wants and desires.

Gary Allman's fundamentals and strategies to unlock your confidence levels in bed. Never be afraid of doing the wrong thing in bed again, for both men and women.

How to transform her into an orgasm machine, by using your mouth only...

... and much more!

Anyone can become a master of Dirty Talk easily and quickly...
you just need to unleash your inner seductive skills and apply
the tactics taught in this book. It's time to let go of the taboo
and embrace the hot, erotic, sensually-exciting world of
Talking Dirty!

This book will teach you how to open up your mouth and voice
what you want, what you love, and exactly how you want it, in
the most attractive way possible. Ready to up your sexual skill
level, improve your sex life and add a little more spice when
the clothes come off? You deserve it!

Amazon.com link: http://amzn.to/2a0vRvK

PS: Do you want to receive a lot of free and bargain books from
the BEST independent authors, every week? You'll get a free
gift too, as soon as you sign up!

Go to: http://bit.ly/28Xaddd

CPSIA information can be obtained
at www.ICGtesting.com
Printed in the USA
LVOW13s2345191217

560343LV00053B/3570/P